SLEEPING LETTERS

SLEEPING LETTERS

MARIE-ELSA R. BRAGG

Chatto & Windus

LONDON

1 3 5 7 9 10 8 6 4 2

Chatto & Windus, an imprint of Vintage,
20 Vauxhall Bridge Road,
London SW1V 2SA

Chatto & Windus is part of the Penguin Random House group of companies
whose addresses can be found at global.penguinrandomhouse.com.

Penguin
Random House
UK

First published by Chatto & Windus in 2019

penguin.co.uk/vintage

A CIP catalogue record for this book is available from the British Library

ISBN 9781784743161

Typeset by EM&EN
Printed and bound in Great Britain by Clays Ltd, Elcograf S.p.A.

Penguin Random House is committed to a sustainable future for
our business, our readers and our planet. This book is made
from Forest Stewardship Council® certified paper.

SLEEPING LETTERS

This book is the expression of an ancient ritual. It was first written over two silent retreats in the mountains: up before dawn, candle lit and waiting by the window. Writing was an act of prayer, Ignatian contemplation, active imagination.

From the beginning I followed blindly, feeling the pain and hope of a love letter, often stalling in fear when, sometimes, there would be the sense of a breeze behind me, the whisper of a voice as if a guide encouraged me to (*step forward*) and face the scene again. Some early readers have called these 'stage directions' and they are right, as both the story and the Liturgy carry the same movement of ritual, which is at the heart of theatre.

Each time a section came to an end, what kept me beside the window was the detailed choreography of performing the Eucharist. From the placement of the altar, to laying out the garments of priesthood and into the service. It gave me a safe place to grieve, rage and find peace while surrounded by the mystery of life in death. And, like the silence after a storm or an act of tenderness, after the sacrament I have always found a stillness.

My story takes place in the two lands my parents

gave me; the fells of Cumbria from my father and the mountains of Provence from my mother. Both landscapes have old churches, often from the twelfth century, near ancient stone circles and cave paintings. And each culture has its tales of hermits, saints and mystics. In these places, for me, nature has been infused with religion; the peaks, lakes and caves as powerful as any cathedral.

The love letter is three-fold. It is to my mother and father, taking us back to the tragedy that happened to our family when I was six years old. Inevitably, it is written to myself allowing the pain to surface, and with brutal honesty it is also a letter to God. The form of conversation follows an elusive thread of memory, myth, lyrical poetry and ritual. Sharing it is exposing, but during my work as a priest and spiritual director, so many have disclosed their lives to me that I offer this simply as someone who stands in the line of a long-held tradition of confession knowing that we are equal and vulnerable, no matter what we have seen and done or not done.

My hope is that readers will find their own path through what follows and that something of my experience waiting by the window is passed on.

SLEEPING LETTERS

She came to my bedroom at night (*step forward*). It was dark, tight as a tail without fur. Tar hoofs drumming across the terrace gardens outside then clipped back to leap over walls and barbed wire. Seagulls stained in hard coal above roofs. She must have brought a chair from her room to sit and talk to me while I was asleep. Hard sleep, my head turned to a glimpse of her – crossed-legged, curls – then falling into my pillow again. Later lifting my face to find her smoking (*look up*), then talking, then it seemed like weeks into the night she came again, might have been there, maybe. Night fermenting. Pools of stained-froth soaking bulrushes and cap moss (*step*), moon fungus fanned to the side of bark. She was putting my heart to rest, hers. Telling me how life would be. How she had found no way out, lost. Broken the last thought, the last. So tired after our long summer in Provence and the flight back. Clouds over the ocean. Waiting for hours at the airport as my father's name was repeated over the loudspeakers. Waiting for him to pick us up like torn packages with extra tax: a stranger watching me on a big chair with my colouring book while she was at the bar.

We drove through London in the back of a taxi, rain drops swollen into small ponds on the windows, each one reflecting the streetlights. Standing together outside our front door as if we were waiting. Key then placed in the lock to the announcement that we would be going to live with Daddy (*step*). Key held still while she waited. Me at her right side. Her, high above and leaning over, eyes watching for a response, which I found, weary-legged, acting a 'Yippee' to be happy for her, so that (*step*) the key could be turned and we would be home. (*Turn to step forward – a blind surrender.*)

We sat in the kitchen across the small wooden table from each other. She ate three Petits Filous yoghurts, I had one. She cried like banks bursting, then silence; like winds blowing through her shoulders, chest bouncing, then long shallow breaths. She ruptured and I watched, silent, emotionless. 'You must stop crying.' 'Yes, you're right.' Sitting straight, hands on laps in front of each other like Russian roulette, like obedient prisoners, like . . . and then her moaning crept in, rising to a heavy tide that's forced down a sheer track, pushing her to splatter round a tight bend, her body jolting forward and she was lost in pain.

'Maman, you must stop crying.'

'Yes.'

She leant back and looked to her knees, arms so pressed

to her sides she was bulbous, breath short and irregular, coughing, holding, spitting to prevent the tears of grief.

'If you don't stop I'll go to bed.'

But she started again, so I walked as loudly as I could up every stair to show that she must stop, and she called, 'Go on then, you just look after yourself,' and I went to bed, to sleep, to bed. This is my confession.

This, is my confession.

ALTAR

**Stone rolled
from the throat of a cave.**

I left.

I sat at the table red-eyed like a patriarchal judge. Each step up the stairs hammered a mallet.

I left.

ALTAR

**Altar carved
out of damp walls.**

Formed in darkness.
Stone, fallen
from dust and gold
to iron.
Chorus in stone.

Now laid
in the centre of the nave
consecrated with water,
salt, ashes and wine
anointed with myrrh,
cinnamon, sweet cane and olive
spread with the bare palm
of a right hand.
Cleansed and censed.

She came to my bedroom; night laid out like a shroud.
Loose eye, loose lip. She returned before she could leave
bringing her chair from another room to talk into my
dreams. Thin voice, translucent, stretched. Ash petal rose.
Night-shroud. Breath-shroud. Flute-cry, owl-cry from the
hills, while pale masks fell like webs over faces, over lips,
taking their print of day.

ALTAR

A carved nook
underneath
filled with relics
tied to word
and then to stone.
A waterspill of blessings.
The awoken fall
and rise of voice.

This is. My confession; my slatted booth, my wood and my coffin. This is my chorus (*to stone*) to sing from and the sight I have found. This is my bones, my earth, my chink, my grave. It's what turns my head to look at the chaos.

This is my fall.

Turn. The kitchen. The stairs. Can't be unravelled brick by brick; regret by forgiveness; love by love; can't change, undo it.

Turn and I'm marked – pillar of salt. Breathe and I'm marked, love and I'm marked. Imagine and I. Pray and.

(*Myrrh in the right hand*) If I don't look, I'll disappear. If I run without seeing, I'll be woven into the mountains till I am scree. I want to run, but bleed to stay. Liquid hope.

ALTAR

Wrapped in linen
Folded and folded
a pleat to each corner.

(*and when we pleat we bind*)

So, I turn: arms sailing like marionette threads ready to be blown. The sky is wider than I think. Orb, cob, funnel, tibular; a wheel of thread. Spiral and weave. A stream of shapes. Look through this and this (*turn*) and the hairs on my neck will rise (*turn*), my wrists and arms will rise. My feet, my thigh, belly and cheek (*spin*), and as my eyes roll back to lined fields spinning white, warm snow, burnished flakes; my psalm is whispered in oh (*turn*) such unexpected sounds, as the veil begins to lift.

CLOTH

Threadbare
and smoothed
over the altar;

pale-streaked
from sun
and Benedictus;

a prayer stitched
under to seal
the tabernacle;

a rabbi's cloak,
its hem trailed
along the ground;

a ragged curtain
to be raised
for the dark theatre

of the formless
shadow-space
beneath the stone.

Scent moves like smoke over the hedge of one garden to the next. It is a distant violin in the day and infuses night.

The filter is thick, but the deeper I breathe, I find that the air was never mine. The gateway is a high arch that widens the closer I move towards it. The craft is to wait minutes, hours, days even years to fill my sight with . . .

There is a thirst
just before dawn;
an afternight of dark sun
behind the line,
iris watching,
an under-bell of purge
that forms the lip
of the inbreath
before song.

CANDLE

Tiers of scored brass
lanterns will be lowered
by a long iron chain,
their slim glass ducts
filled with olive oil,
the new pale flax wicks
curling as they drink.

A wax taper will be lit
from the paschal candle
and cupped to the lamps
until their saffron haze
is hoisted to a half-fallen,
half-raised crown
above the glowing altar.

(and when we pleat we bind.
Crossing through and under
linen with crushed rose and bark
new stems with bud. Water.)

I don't know how I'm going to show you dawn was closed, like the inside of an egg; further away now, can see the back of it. Show you that I sat on the top step, knees together. Felt like there was a river under the stairs. My small head leaning cold against the wall, soaking in the white, pooling. Top step, knees up like a fence to the dark side of the house, past night, no dawn. That's the way it was, dark on the house side, white wall on the other. Waking to sticky grey, to lost, to the closed door of her room, to no slipping into her bed for our morning doze, rattling the handle, rhythmic and metal-loud like trains on a railway track. Air crawling downstairs, smoulder-slow. Moving no further than the top step; my mother's door behind me. My eyes stinging, looking into the house from the side, as if around a corner, the closest to straight my shoulders would allow, shadow spreading.

You can taste it when you breathe: old breath, last breath, dust.

Wall side, house side (*jump*). Night of house side closing tight with the shine of a black nut.

> – jump, high, shins up, fingers splayed
> – dart, a shadowed gazelle
> backlit on the horizon,
>
> let height ignite my eyes, black, onyx, jet,
> – everything is smaller, my cup is
> smaller, the drink is smaller, my thirst is
>
> smaller. My dance is, my dance is,
> rounder, further across the fields
>
> if I could see you walking
> it would be from inside your shoes
>
> jump into the tide – and fight, choke,
> nose dribbling, no air, no – cry;
> beat the dull bells in your hands – jump

COLLAR BOX

The black bible-leather
collar box is embossed
with the Magnificat
and wings of fire.
When I open the lid
a rim of bone lies coiled
in the mute dark,

a double pleat
of black cotton
and white canvas,
its centre open
like harbour walls,
two strong black
pillars of prayer;

the white space
an unwritten text,
the moment before
and the moment after,
a stillness of plainsong,
a torn sheet
raised in surrender.

*(and we pleat to bind, covered and bare,
young hand with old. Water)*

The house was drowning in dirty water, stagnant. Too thick for a child to carry a fish down the hall in her arms, to bend a glowing pike at the window; fins from candle-carp slicing the roof. No clear water shells at my feet or red starfish in chalky silt ponds on the shore where I could pour small bottles of paint – red, blue and green – and watch them curl as if they swam, as if they were alive. Water too thick for ships, for sunken foghorns to bleat, for wood carved with tiny nails. Or if there were any ships, they had charcoal boughs, built in the dark with charred wood from abandoned fires, drawing black snail trails as they sliced through the floors. It's hard to tell from the top of the stairs, that's just the way it was; right side seeping into white paint, soggy wall slipped like old skin from lime. Wallpaper holes leaching through to plaster, to sand, never seaside, never to the other side; my small head tilted as if it were piled to the side. That's the way the wall was. That's the way the front door stood, tight at the end of the hall, never alight like a lamp, only silver-lit like an old neon sign thrown into tin.

I walked away.
I hid.
Obedient.

I don't know how I can call you to move three paces forward, and three paces forward. It's easier than two. Harder than four; but you get lost in four, it is too folded, too purposeful, too neat.

That's the way the wall seeped, soaking streaks of white into me. House shadow closing my left eye, bass-tone silent.

> – jump – Now – alive through the day,
> clattering into night, scared bullock, legs splayed
> – jump – a crack to the wind,
>
> chin up, face leaning back as if there is sun
> – shiver the grass, crack the oak, bramble,
> thorn. Let berries scrape your side – jump –
>
> off the path into pine and cedar
> holding their leaves like boats to the air
> – canter wildly, knees up, throat knotted – jump.

ROBES

I lay out the cope
with its ladder of roses

then pleat my stole
to an alpha incipit

I drape my alb
like two sleeping wings

with the knotted cincture
gathered as a harness

I lay the thin amice
with its cords crossed and doubled

and my heavy black cassock
arms folded to the heart

its thirty-three buttons
in a long bound cascade

for each told and untold
year of Christ's life

(through and under)

Morning is pale and cracked like old cream varnish, like eggs now blown too hard: pink sac stretched to translucent, clinging; maybe lit inside. Carpet on the stairs has fermented through the night. Seeds have sprouted and thin-stemmed grass has pushed through, pressed around dirty toes, clawed nails, peat webs. My jaw has grown large to the right; leant on too long, gaping. It hangs heavy and bovine, crystal dribble to the chin. A crunch and snap in my right ear and into the skull when I try to close it, teeth out of line. Grass is high to the wall, woven in like catchweed. White poppies have grown from my right palm, snow drops and white crocus from my right knee, my thigh. White foxgloves to my right shoulder, white iris in my right eye, salt in my left. No hand but charred wood to my left arm, tree bark to the left side of my stomach. Moss and swamp from the carpet must have soaked into my left shin and grown my leg long overnight – or was it more than one night? Left heel pressed through carpet, through stair, into broken boards and empty floor next to tins, cigarette butts, shavings and dust. Roots in the sole of my foot uninterested in ground, knotting together to form bundles, to form clumps; clubfoot, burr, trunk.

We all walked away, mouths open. Obedient, blind. Three in a row. Kissed, betrayed, kissed, betrayed.

(and the song)

> rumbles in low chant
> with coal-mallet throats.
> And the song shakes
>
> across the fields
> with its threshing tide;
> a blade of whispers

that urges us to listen –
then bolts, a burst of wings
wide over the forests,

laughing. And the song is, and the song is
that the floors in our homes are forests
carved into an offering
that we walk on

that the glass in our hand
is fire-blown rock
lifted for us to drink,

that grace is dripped
into our mouths,
hovering over us.

My mother was found in the afternoon. Split door. Torn frame. When they talked about seeing her laid out like that, they said she had meant it.

She'd left the keys with the old lady next door. Peggy, strong-footed in plimsolls. She lived on her own and worked as an administrator at school. My mother told her she had to leave because of an urgent telegram and asked her to give me breakfast. Must have forgotten that I came into her bed before dawn. Peggy striding in, annoyed by my noise: I had built into waves – times of exhaustion and no breath – then a trace of energy like the light from one match, which I would fight to use for the highest scream – forest and undergrowth seen through a chink of light – then I'd slump again against the wall. By 8 a.m. she took me next door (*stone rolled*), pale and quaking, for cornflakes without sugar. Then I was delivered to my friend's house. We lay on a sofa by the back garden, my head on her six-year-old lap. Adults moving about and talking intensely in the front kitchen. My friend stroking my sweaty hair, me unable to see or hear. It was her father who found my mother. When he talked about it later in my life he had such reverence and respect for her, saying she had left nothing to chance. He became someone I watched for how to live.

By evening, my father arrived and took me to the front pew of a church, held me on his knees and told me my mother wasn't coming back. He wept with more melody than she had, a deeper moan, wet nose and face. He held on to my arms and buried his cheek into my neck. His body hunched as if it might crack.

> Red roses, storm roses,
> torn tongues. They rust
> and count, swarmed.
> No first. Scent repeating.

BELL

With a bare grip I pull the rough flaxen rope
and bow my length from head to thigh
for the swing of the iron flight
of the clapper tongue
in its mouth
to toll

and I'm winched towards the roof
arms stretched, to hang, to trust

the jolt
the plunge
the wing, the easing
of my grip as the rope leaps
to catch the weight of the new fall
which I will clasp, pulling to the ground

My mother and I were marked by the mistral from
the beginning. It seared the backs of our heels two or
three times a year (*lean*) like a wild spiral ladder, scarring
its name into our souls as a painter would the edge of its
canvas. Marie-Elsa Mistral; Marie-Elisabeth Mistral. Two
winds that meet twice a year after months of betrothal.
Their yearning feeds our soil. And when they meet –

from the high Bay of Biscay to the west and the low Gulf of Genoa to the east – they rise and fall like great wings stretching the roots of the oak shrub and its closed-eye tops to ecstatic prayer. But in the delight of meeting, their love becomes blind passion and reaches to such a blaze that, unaware, they draw a third iced stream of dust wind from the north, which furiously tunnels through the valleys to veil and quench our peaks, reciting the love songs of Icarus as he fell from the sun.

THURIBLE

The chain will be held high in the left hand,
and low in the right, where a copper dome
has star-holes which the links run through.
The lid of the dome will be lifted, and pulled
along its chains with a rattle to the top;
leaving the base open like a half egg
showing the secret before it was formed.

Oh Maman, it's hard to write – and would dismantle me to do,
*(*lean forward*) but I would like to sit with you at the kitchen*
table again. Even though the wood now seems splintered. I
didn't see your funeral – open coffin with roses. I saw a day

when people weren't there and came back tired. Though I don't know if I would have survived seeing you in death. The sight of you closed. No matter how tender the red petals around you. The shock of not being able to make you feel better. I think I would have run down the aisle in my best red shoes to wake you up; clutch your death mask; been defiantly pulled off you. Then shutdown; though that happened anyway. I nearly stopped speaking. It would have been a relief to stop speaking. But it would have been like walking up the stairs away from Pa, and I could never do that again.

Up the road from me there are two churches with plain glass windows (lid of the dome). If you walk in the middle of the road you can see through both churches to sky on the other side. Like a telescope aligning. Lead squares bringing the focus. I went once at night, needing to see through to the other side, but couldn't tell if I saw night or if the windows were too dark.

(and the song is)

And when the northern dust of the mistral brings three days of constant darkness, silencing the cicadas, it is said that you can hear a low chorus, especially resonant in the many caves around Mount Ventoux and Mount Lure, where Icarus healed for years as a hermit. But this chorus is too endless to remember. Its vowels are long, reaching into the inner wells and waterlines, and the consonants can be as precise as percussion, their formulas repeating as if poetry and geometry were the same craft.

The old women in our village used to say that this chorus was in fact the chant Icarus used for his return to the sun, bathed equally as he ascended in earth and sea. They say it's the reason our vines produce good wine; that a couple whose rings are placed overnight on a stone from our caves will discover a good marriage is to be taken in slowly, and that the songs of the hermit change the air, so that our church bells are heard further than their iron would send. My mother was a painter. She painted Icarus again and again. She used my father as the model for his body.

Maman, did you search for your mother in lithography and paint
Did you search for her like a myth

THURIBLE

Charcoal will be placed inside the bowl:
three small circles of pressed dust. A taper
held close until they burn with a purple corona,
while a small bronze spoon will crack them open
to be breathed on, until their grasp
becomes a bite, and then a pulse.

My father told me that my grandmother died suddenly from an infection two weeks after my mother was born, and so she was given to a Parisian orphanage. All babes laid together in white, waiting for their mothers to return from the clay (*placed inside*). My mother's parents were biologists, so my grandmother's story was always bound with the lament that penicillin was not yet available, so the infection in her sinuses spread like bushfire to her pituitary gland (*a taper held close*). I have a photograph of her three days after my mother's birth: she's tilting her baby towards the camera with delight in a silk white bow, a vase of roses by the bed, her aunt doting. I keep it next to a small square picture of my grandmother in her white coat sitting at her laboratory desk with test tubes and a microscope. After becoming a mother, she returned to work for just under a week.

We were given to our fathers, Maman, watching them, unsure
if women use the same tools.

I used to dream of my grandmother travelling to
Mexico to search for orchids as proof of paradise. She was
brought up with a view of the Botanical Garden in Paris
after generations of her family had travelled through
Russia and Poland: intricate passageways I've not been
able to trace. Her familiarity with being an outsider was
put to use when she was one of the first women to go
to university in France and study science. I'm not sure if
she was allowed the official degree. I am sure, however,
that the disapproval of male academia was akin to facing
a Minotaur.

Did you visit the gardens by your mother's home
Did you imagine her planting new lilies and orchids; counting
species
Did you learn to survive with the precision and abandon of an
explorer

THURIBLE

Knots of pale myrrh-sap from torchwood bark
pierced with its own thorn will be brought
in a bronze myrtle boat and heaped
onto the small central pit of charcoal
to simmer in white smoke as thick as paint.

My grandfather was born above a karst spring in Sorgue. By the sound of water spilling from river caves. If they dried into hunger karsts, he could enter; cracked clay skin at his feet, comb pillars shadowing the tunnels. Before I was born, my grandfather bought the ruins of a waterhole in a medieval mountain village. Blue, yellow and green pigment ridges climbing up towards us from the ochre valley of Rustrel. Three tall cypress trees in the garden and a round opening in the kitchen floor to check on the animals below. Walls so wide they cling to the rock by weight instead of foundations. On either side of the fire in his study were two large urns from a shipwreck off the coast of Java. They were covered in waves of barnacles. And the shelves and cupboards around his desk were filled with fragments of Roman pots, cuneiform tablets and slabs of hieroglyphics with cartouches scattered down them like beads. When he died, I found an old box of medals and ceremonial keys to the universities he had worked with. Each had a symbol or a face: Thoth ibis scribe of Cairo, cedar tree of Lebanon, a profile of Frederick III of Bonn, the spires of Oxford, an eagle of St Petersburg, the key to the Sorbonne. My uncle thought of giving them to an artist to melt into a sculpture. Maybe a tree. Maybe a cave. When I now sit at his desk watching swifts dart into the evening thermals, medals and clay behind me, I remember his tales of his great uncle Jean-François who was allowed into Napoleon's hoards from Egypt, crouching into corners obsessively trying to understand hieroglyphics, until one day he flew ecstatic along the streets of Paris to his brother's office only to faint from the heights of trying to describe how he had cracked the code. My grandfather fought to fly forward, believing he moved with past generations like cliff swallows migrating in formation, sheltering from the wind, sharing the apex. He had two types of photographic memory. Stories in cinematic detail. The memory of his first wife and of my mother must have been overwhelming.

Did you find mother in charcoal life drawings
mother in statues
mother in prose

THURIBLE

The lid will be steered down the chains,
taut from the weight of the coals,
the dome unevenly caught, grating, hanging,
a reckoning sound to its fall,
until it locks into the lip of the bowl,
and a gold ring gathers the chains over the stars
so that all can be swung, link-spindle to sphere,
a pendulum lung: smoke sucked into the holes
through the arc of the swing and exhaled at its peak.

Did you find mother in poetry,
in perfume
mother in liturgy

In the cover of night, my grandfather met a colleague in the grounds of the University of St Petersburg. His friend had got hold of a rusted ring of keys and they snuck out to see forbidden Orthodox churches, unlocking heavy wooden doors to altars, chapels and paintings in handheld candlelight with equal surprise and scrutiny. When he told me, he looked across the table to the kitchen wall in awe; names, dates, historical and scientific detail falling from him like the chatter of a stream. I only noticed the sound of the words, the meanings were too fleeting for me to grasp, but I could feel a wide dusty space between the circular archways and see the pink cheek and blue cloak of a gilded painting.

Did you know the timidity of a scapegoat
lose your name, your voice
become damp
Did you get caught, arms and throat scraped, in a silent crown
of thorns

Just before he died, we went for a walk in the mountains. Always the same route, same suit, stick in hand. Some of the lavender harvest had fallen from a truck and, when he saw my delight, he stepped forward and, completely out of character, laid his walking stick into a large bundle and, full armed, belly out, chin and staff to the sunset, carried it home. We stopped three times. At first we sat on the bank by the path and he told me that it would be a valuable deed if, when I was older, I researched the kidneys, because they were more central in the body's health than was recognised.

Did you find Mother in the theatre
in Piaf Chansons

The second time we sat in silence (*pleat*), and the third time we watched the valley in its lantern glow of after-sun, when he said, with such effort it gave a kind of humble ceremony, that he loved my grandmother and my mother, but, eyes welling towards Mount Lure, he had never told my mother, so he wanted to tell me that he loved me.

THURIBLE

The chains are in the left hand, ring in the right;
the globe hangs like fire-fruit to cense the altar
with its bronze veil opening and closing behind,
before it soars into a Benedictus
three times three to the left,
three times three to the right,
three to the Cross, three to the Cross,
its smoke still reaching while it returns
to a sound that will not be
the tide of money or jailer's keys,
not the scales of justice or a spurred salute.

Maman, if I could send you a letter, you would unfold the paper to find fine slices of shells and dried grasses from our walks woven into a thin veil of your mother's white lace.

Did you find mother in dance
in an icon
in the Church

Do you remember the mountains taking us in like tributaries, the two of us gleaning as we climbed, picking prickled stems of dry flowers and grasses? We'd let the light roll us out of bed, no curtains, and go without cleaning our teeth, scrambling over rock and itchy brush, ochre staining our shins, finding a steady rhythm once our breath was deep into a heavy pant. We clambered like mountain goats, a slice of view between tree, between breath, our bodies waving across the boulders like wind in grass. And then – 'Ah, another garden.' A piece of open settled ground, and we would stop to take in the valley with solidity, as if the rock behind us gave the feeling of looking out of a house. Our home. The enclave forming us. The cicadas leaving the beat of our feet and reaching skyward. Our spines straightening again as if this were a history we belonged to. Dry leaves folded like star-cups becoming familiar. And then we would be off again.

Do you remember the long reed stems that were cavernous and bulged at their tops, as wide as tabernacles, and their knotted

leaves that stood like statues ready to speak – and how we
hooked them into our belts; clusters of tall strangers, their
ruffled crowns wrapped into the linen on our backs; and that
by late morning our ties of cloth were so full of dried flowers,
it was as if they swaddled us, rustling like paper bells on our
posied climb?

Ah, you're painting now, lifting your chin, eyes closed to the
breeze. It's like the moment before laughing. We're still there,
you and I, something of us at least is in the mountains, in
the abandoned ruins and caves, in the bleached boulders, the
crevices full of winding wooded rosemary stems firing their
dark green into the night. We're careful with the white sun and
wary of summer fires, each longing to slip into the evenings
between the warm ochre soil, our hearts cracked open to the
sky, and sleep.

On Mount Lure I found a cave
with the faint print of a woman.
I noticed her hands first,
as if she pushed through the wall,
as if she waited, as if she blessed.

She reminded me of Pasiphae
and her daughter Ariadne.
Of a labyrinth made for maddening love,

of shame earned and unearned,
a thread given to follow by touch.

Of Mary and Elisabeth in revelation,
their wombs on fire with ecstatic love.
Of Mary Magdelene pushing through
the myth of her stoning, to wait
in the garden and pass on her discipleship.

And then I saw the slave girl, mother
of Icarus. A shadow woman standing
in the charcoal pit of the cave
ready to move towards the tunnel
and light from the unwritten day.

THURIBLE

It will be the sound of nails creaking into bud
and the folding of golden skin.
It will be the sound of breath in the harmonium,
the creak between keening and laughter
like veins of a gold river spilling its links.

Maman, there's always something more, something missing
about that night (veins of a river). Through my teenage
years a wondering would creep up on me in the street and I

would search for the back of your head, curls or scarf, square shoulders. Or I would look to the far corner of a road, thinking you might be standing there watching me, as if you had returned, finally been released from an asylum. I knew you broke under the despair of a silenced woman, lost in gaslight, your heart easier to destroy than listen to – and I thought you might come back healed. Wait outside the house. See how I'd grown, what I looked like when I walked (passing where we pleat again).

Did you think Icarus ended up in the Labyrinth because his father dismissed his mother as 'slave girl'? Did he fly from pain in search of divine mother? Was his elation beautiful because it had pain alongside the joy? Did he disobey the rules because he learned to ignore his father's rough magic – made a fevered bid for a world without lies (tears running down his beard)? Did he leap to merge with the sun, no spirits whispering in his ear (if I were human)? No circle of forgiveness. Or was it a compulsion, thin skin on the palms of his hands, a vicious escape, craving heat, wings beating the air for inspiration to merge? And were your paintings of your fall or my father's?

All I had was the picture of you from the back of your novel, and that only a few years later when I found it on a shelf. Pa had your watercolours, some photos and drawings of you in his study. Some in his desk drawer. It would have been so different *to have had a painting of yours and some photographs in my bedroom. It was as if I wasn't allowed to think of you.*

*Your friends have all confessed to me over the years (*lean forward*). Guilty of 'not doing enough to help', 'not realising,' 'not coming over that night when you called'. They still love you as if you've only just died. I know Jay came over to see you that night. She said you were broken by Pa's infidelity, his refusal to face a divorce. So much can be said in anger and when we are entangled, we believe it. You felt invaded. Tutu told me that during our last summer, Pa sent a package to Provence and you wouldn't open it thinking it might be a bomb. Your brother Michel told me that Pa threatened to take me from you. I've made myself face that kind of pain out of some kind of respect for your truth. Back in London, Jay said you'd left thread across the doorways, so you would know if he'd secretly been in the house while you were away. And they hung by the doors (*right hand held out*).*

Caroline came over late that evening and sat on your bed, talking – she can only remember that you were upset, but not about to break. Carol and Alistair's neighbour told them we had turned up to stay, suitcases in hand, but they were away. Sheila talked to you on the phone, but couldn't come, like Joan and Cecilia. You called Pa who said he would come in the morning. The last question you asked him was, 'Do you think I'm a good mother?'

HANDS

A glass bowl and jug
stand ready
I pour three streams
on to each palm
three on the back of my hands,
while the empty bowl
becomes full.

(crossing through and under)

A few years ago, I put a bench on Hampstead Heath for you with a simple prayer carved into the wood. From it, you can watch autumn colours in the valley falling to a red-brick bridge. A haze of bud and spring.

Once it was placed, I invited Pa (both hands held out) and he came with your wedding ring. He wept, could hardly speak, trying to tell me how you bought it together on Portobello Road.

About six months later I was at a lecture on Jewish mysticism and someone spoke about the Shekinah. She said she had followed a sense of grace one Sabbath across the Heath through woods, across muddy streams, into thicket and strange paths till she came to a bench with an old Kabbalistic prayer on it, which she read out – it was yours (I kept quiet!):

> 'Eternally holding soul
> Catch the dew of heaven
> And blossom'

Another three months later I was in a Hampstead café and a group of young people on the table next to me arranged to meet at 'the lover's bench', giving directions to yours!

The following year, Pa called asking for the chapter and verse of the Bible passage on your bench, because an Oxford professor of Hebrew sat there regularly and had been through every page, but couldn't find it.

Did you find mother in ritual
the rim and the wine

Years later someone went to the trouble of getting a small brass plaque, having it inscribed, walking around a fallen tree to the bench and, tools in their pocket, they screwed it tightly under my prayer:

> 'O how fortunate to have awakened
> such sweet passion'

I have no idea who it was.

COLLAR

**I will bow
before I take a circle
of white silence
to my throat
for the Song
and a circle
of black silence
to my voice
for the Word**

(and when we pleat we bind)

I colour my hair like you did, enjoying the wet time when it sets, and I speak with my hands. I've lived a creative way of life and love searching conversations. I laugh a lot when life is going well. Don't smoke like you did, but I do hum around the house. Did you hum? Grandma did. I like to read and sometimes draw a shape before I find the words. There are things I don't know. After you left, Grandma patted my back for hours till I slept. She sang to me. When she wasn't there to put me to bed, I wet the sheets. Lived with the bitter smell of old urine. I think Pa loved you more after you died. Was loyal to keeping you alive. I'd like to tell you that you have always been with me like a scent. But often I've turned away from you from fear of what happened. I'm sorry I turned away. Fear makes me cower instead of bow. I think I have always linked love and death. Never found the fulcrum of Christ's death. Always watching for it. If I have a child, I might read to them in the early hours to infuse their dreams. Or leave small gifts for the morning. I would like to read The Little Prince *like you did, but I will allow the repetition of the fox if they ask for it!*

It's hard to end a letter when the desire to talk to you is in my skin. But I do want to know if you found women – Jay, Cynthia, Margaret, Mary, Elsie – who stood in the place – Ethel, Hannah, Margaret, Elsie, Barbara, Mary, Poh-Sim – of mother.

CASSOCK

I put on the cassock
and its weight
will hold me,
present and solemn
in the constant toll
of an old river bell
as I page the streets
with a hearse at my back,
as I walk the aisle
with the Cross at my back,
into kitchens and wards

with the dove at my back,
while desert sand trails
from its old worn hem.

Pa, I know you can't think about Maman without pain (reach).
In the years after she died, when I came back from school, I
didn't feel at home until I climbed the stairs to your study with
an apple and black coffee, waiting till you finished writing to sit
quietly on your knee in the comfy chair. You, often crying into
the nook of my shoulder. Both looking up to Maman's small
square pencil drawings – one of her, one of you.

Did you find wife in writing?
in exploring the craft of composers, dancers, painters, sculptors?
Did you find sun in their eyes?

Thank you for talking about her as if you could see through
the wall to a place where she still lived, your heart lifting,
brow mesmerised, slipping into confusion then disbelief as if
you were in conversation with the vision of her. Thank you for
talking about her family as if they were treasure. Thank you for
walking in the Colorado by Rustrel as if the Impressionists were
still collecting pigment, their easels fixed in the mountains, and
for visiting Maman's family and friends to talk into the night
about fossils, authors and world affairs.

Did you find mother in the red soil?
in the night?

I remember that sometimes in Provence you would look warm,
as if you had been sitting in the sun with Maman for hours, but
mostly you could hardly bear being so close to memories of her,
your eyes welling up by the front door, 'Come on now Marie-
Elsa, off to bed,' before you set off to walk for hours.

Do you think that if we paint ourselves clean, ignoring the
dirt, we always feel a deceit? The varnish of an imposter? If
people can't see what we've done, does the fraud make us lose
faith in the cleanse? Does claiming innocence help us remember
a full heart?

Pa, I think that you kept her things close in your study, outside
time, because anywhere else they were in danger of being in the
past (from its old worn hem)*. Maybe you've been trying to*
find her all these years.

(we bind)

When you wrote a novel about her, I asked if the old wooden
chest you described full of photos and letters that you couldn't
open was real.

Do you survive by being in continual flight?

*I confess, when I was a child I often went through your desk
drawers to find the shells she'd painted. To be close to you while
you were away at work; sit on your chair near her paintings.
But I never really noticed the chest. It was just there.*

AMICE

**The linen
is folded
in three
and wrapped
around my neck;
the straps
crossed
at my heart
and my back,
tied
at my belly;
a quiet
wing
at my throat.**

*I was shocked when you said it was true and that you couldn't
bear me seeing inside. It's hard to say, but when you were away*

I stole into your room and saw it as if for the first time. Brown oak (crossed at my heart). The long size and shape of a coffin. Frightened to open the lid. Somehow racing back down the aisle at the funeral. And there she was. Happy with me playing in the park; smoking and laughing at you in the garden; sitting on a rock with dark, summer-brown skin and wild hair, looking out over the sea. A long letter about her beliefs. Negatives of her watching me in her knitted poncho again. More than framed memories.

And when you continually fall, do you believe you deserve the pain or that torture is an inevitable price for the sun?

I'm sorry for going into your study like that. I tried to tell you what I'd done a few times, but sat across the kitchen table from you worried that somehow, if you knew I had seen her there, in the chest, there would be no barrier to your grief. You did everything you could to stop sinking and I did everything I could to never again leave the table and walk away.

I see our imagination creates, brings the invisible to life, but have you found that, like the prodigal son, it returns us to grace

> And still some women return
> to the round, broken and re-tied,

filling the corners of the cave
to surround the hermits
who lie with heavy rocks on their eyes.

Women kneeling, a circle of twelve
and twelve and twelve. One becoming
a fury of scolding truths from the pit,
another surfacing with an echo-song
from the seam of a river, another

painting the ceiling with paradise
or planting the veins of earth
while some claw back from their fall,
all repairing the circle as they kneel again
like ancient rock prints, sitting vigil.

Oh Maman, it must have been a relief to find an analyst who was from Provence. A rare and bold woman in the Jungian world. Her father raised only a few towns away from yours. The two of you smoking and talking in your mother tongue past the hour (and when we bind, we bow). That day when you rang the bell for your session and there was no reply, did you wait? You heard nothing for weeks, but told no-one – where did you go? (a quiet wing) What did you do? Did you walk, lost in the gardens of London?

My mother's therapist was called Anne Darquier. She discovered that her father was not the town doctor like his father before him, as she had been told, but organised yellow stars and trains for Jewish citizens to be sent to camps. Forty years later, another of her patients, Carmen Callil, wrote a book about Anne, explaining that she had died from an accidental overdose of sleeping pills, pain-killers and alcohol. But at the time people were told it was suicide. Anne died six months before my mother.

Let it be that on my evening walk past the Rotonde to the chapel above the village I feel the mirage of you warm by my side as if you visit from time to time to talk (with the bronze veil opening). That we peer into the ruin of the vicarage with the damson tree, taller every year, and gaze from that inner garden out through its three windows to fig leaves in the light beyond. Elderflower as thick as honeycomb clinging from hearth to beam with its resonant hum. And let us sit by the well at the edge of the chapel garden with its fallen wall, watching Mount Lure (a circle of silence) as if we were carefully rocked by the valley through the evening.

I throw the alb
like an open sail
and step under

praying to the momentary
rush of the Holy Spirit
falling around me

quick to stretch
the width of the Cross
into its long sleeves

Maman, I'm worried about Pa (width of the cross). *If the Helm Wind is afoot in the Cumbrian fells, he'll head out into it as it screeches down from the Pennines like a chariot rider on a standing wave of cloud. Sapphire eye at the ready. Whinnying grey horses gathered to the starting line across the peaks. White bulls bent for the chase. Wheels within wheels. He'll brace himself, collar up, heading into the steel sheets of rain, furrowed brow, pacing, watching for lightning, and the rattling uplift of the start gates. The fury of the race is in him. The strike. Pounding through the tight wreath of heather gathered around the summits with its threaded knot of rose and swollen roots dug in like a bass tone braced for the shrill thrashing. It's the pain of wife and mother in him, the dark-lit oil, and his flight can be furious.*

My Cumbrian grandmother (*reach like an open sail*) was called Mary Ethel. Song-mother. Beloved lullaby, day trip, hand-holding while watching TV, 'Stand tall', new dress every Christmas, and would you like some more chips in newspaper with a pickled egg, mother. She called my name as if it were a ballad. As a child she regularly passed a quiet woman in the street – toddlers' new shoes, skipping shoes, school shoes – possibly knowing she was a house-maid for one of the big houses on the hill, but it wasn't until my grandmother was eleven that she found out the woman was her mother. She'd become pregnant twice without a husband, probably by an abusive employer. She managed to avoid a place in an asylum for the madness of giving birth outside wedlock and spent her life protecting her two daughters from the workhouse. Until the day she died she had the strength to continue working to pay for two foster carers to look after her children. Wing-maker. Thread-bearer, gatekeeper. Later, when my father was a boy, she visited him once a year. He only remembers being left in a silent room with a 'strong-featured woman in black', who then gave him a half crown.

My Cumbrian grandfather's mother died from TB when my grandfather was seven. One year older than I was when Maman died. He knew how to hold me safe on his knee. She died just as the Maryport coal pit collapsed under the Irish Sea, trapping her husband. His second wife, great-grandmother Hannah, and my grandfather's sisters – Mary, Elsie and Margaret – kept me by their sides, baking, painting, chatting, praying, cleaning.

In the end my grandmother died on the Silloth Solway just by the sea. The day they stopped giving her water and she went into a coma I brought her a bunch of dog roses from the dunes – 'Look, Grandma, aren't they beautiful? I've brought you some sea roses' – and to the nurses' gasps she opened her eyes, struggling to focus on the wide puce petals and smiled with the delight of a child. A week before, in London, someone knocked at my door in the night. I searched, but there was no one there (*reach*). They knocked again and again through the early hours, calling me to the door until I walked along the road and into the garden with a torch. At 7 a.m. my father phoned to say Grandma had nearly died that night, but was settled now, no need to worry. I drove straight to her and found she had sunk into memories, reliving the traumas and hopes, the conversations. I knew the sound of her voice so well that when she talked, questioning a situation, meeting someone, distressed, I replied as the other person or a companion, often without many words, but with a tone of voice that fit her memories. At one point she crossed her hands over her chest, 'Never, never, never, never,' and I knew it was her grief about my mother (*and when we reach, hand open, we bow*). Later she called out for

her own mother and I got into bed and held her as she
had held me when I was a child. Motherless, motherfull.

we are all bound
all bound and generations give no real
separation. We can forget, but it surfaces
as gift to our children and great-grandchildren,
soon losing any recognisable shape,
all fated to cling to each other
and sink or fly.

Let the mistral come like fire crackling along the outline
of Mount Lure (*beat, beat the ground*); let boulders leap
into the sand. Red dust, snake eye, let it rain upwards,
let it rain upwards from the land and let the boiling fit
of rubble grow as streaks of sun reach between their
drum, closer now. Rocks with their matted hair and leath-
er-strong skin climbing over the mountain from the east.
Let the Desert Mothers come, let them be hundreds, bare
and clothed. Let the Desert Mothers answer this pain, let
their circles break and rebuild. Crystal shriek, wolf whine,
fox scream, mother's wail, daughter's roar, let them keen
into the night and start fires in the caves to burn creeping and lemon thyme, praecox mother thyme, and let

them answer. Let them come dust-ridden, life-streaked, skin-written and let them answer. Take the night, take the night to write your liturgical songs with blood and water on the walls. Let your sand paintings be hands in their thousands forming streaks of calcite into the rock pools, pushing into void and crevice. Write your lives in dust on the floor, then spill the wine over it thirty-nine times and turn (*step forward*) each one of you into the pit and look, lean, reach, stare towards the tunnel. Let the ropes be untied; the straitjackets torn away. Let the rusted chains be beaten into submission until they crack, and when it is yours, when it's yours, let each one of you walk, climb, scramble to the foot of the new-lit cave and give us your song. Where is your song?

CINCTURE

The rope
of the cincture
will be tied
in the loop-knot
of a penitent:
twice round my waist,
one bowline
to my right and one

bowline to my left
for my stole
to hang through.

When I look for the truth of that night, Maman, I find frag-
ments and fantasy. Even hidden memories have their own life
and change with the years. If I succumb to a fantasy of you, the
peace I find doesn't feel shared between us; there's no embrace,
only a passing rest. No strength beyond our fates. The strain of
need corrupts my sight. Sometimes I return to the table with you
to watch, to find truth in my love. But I bring the ravaging years
after your death with me. It seeps like an oil slick, a hemlock of
shame, as if I'm imprisoned so far from light that my wounds
devour me. I know that shame is mine, but I wonder if your fall
was tainted in the same way. Stained and unworthy. Recently,
I watched as if the table were a wooden cross laid between us
and I saw myself, six years old, trying to become larger than
life, wider than the winds, rounder than the virgin, bolder than
the thunder of justice to face the barren desolation that was
shattering you. And now – only to silence reporters who wanted
me to prove you didn't jump out of a window – I've just read
your death certificate. I've seen what pills you took after we
faced each other at the table, after the stairs and the sleep. I feel
small in front of the official print. It's toxic to read. But I know
I must or I will lose the love. And now I find myself wondering

what would happen to your soul if you were given a chance to read it. The sight of it burns me.

What happens to creative flight
when imagination is fuelled,
a faulty valve,
pistons rattling
from the pressure of madness.
Do some fly higher
because they no longer know the shape of a wing,
while others feel the heat
of hell and mistake it for sun.

STOLE

Before I put on the stole
I will kiss the Cross
at the nape of its neck
and then place the Cross
and the kiss on mine.

Maman, when I was so ill, on the brink of death, I felt stretched between worlds. Pulled between the mountains of Elisabeth and

the fells of Mary. The Mistral and the Helm. No chance, no
energy to waste on fantasy – just cold, unknown fate. As if I
was left with only the hyphen in my name across the Celtic Sea.
A stretcher without a body. Mourner's linen for the unknown,
unbinding and unbinding. A woman confined to the balcony of
mist, while night prayers were chanted in the waves. A lone arm
in the crowd reaching to touch His hem.

If I find the hand of God
will it be wrapped in a stained poultice and gauze
that I recognise, will the fingers and palm
be free underneath; body above the altar
breaking from the Cross, nails falling
with splinters and dust as the arms reach

COPE

The cope is an oval
of watered silk
placed on my shoulders
like a glass monstrance
for the giving of bread,
a tear half-fallen.

Pa, I have fought to live life as if love were at its centre:
returned to, so that nothing could take me from its path, its
bloom. To fall was to find a wiser love. To sacrifice for love
was to prove that within our broken, spilt, tainted pain we can
remain full. I've seen people turn away from love to achieve
their bright embroidered suit and end as empty as those who
have had no choice but to close the shell of their soul. And I
have learnt that brokenness, even cruelty, is to be loved, though
with care not to fall into the abyss. But, Pa, it has to be that
among all these broken wings there is something more than the
fight for love.

OFFERING

I am in the early light, softening the jointed stems
of sweet reed grass to bend without angle,
letting their heads shiver and trail to the side,

thatching in fox sedge and creeping bent,
spike rush speared through like a high-held note
and vernal grass, purple husk after purple husk,

all needles and fur-sheaths woven in,
all child, all woman, woven and bound,
all plaited in patches of down-seed and glint.

The yew in the woods is as dark and hollow as a well
wound with ivy and wild honeysuckle, their stamens
falling like rain, a tabernacle of low brush,

a yew-crypt, silent under midday cloud.
I lay my bundle on the rust of last year's pine
and push it forward through needles, bark and earth,

and there I drift into sleep like an old woman
beside her reed swathe of letters,
wondering if it would be in the burning or burying

that she would remember what was written,
almost given, almost broken, almost given,
waking by an ancient arch opening to an aisle of light

which I enter to gather bark and grasses again
with hook and eye, a cleaver sting in my palms,
a mud-rash of moss, an under-net of leaves.

At the line of trees I step out into the afternoon
and am the wing of field and marsh, simmering
towards the sea, a clear drink of sap in the waves,

which I stoop to join, my bundle filled with
sow thistle, harebell, cranesbill, speedwell,
meadowsweet, cross heath, bee orchid and vetch.

The beach along the Solway is marked
with driftwood and the silver flames of sand sedge,
each bare towards the sea

and folded into my gift like ornaments,
my sheaf then placed just beyond the tideline
where I wait, whispering compline into the night,

while the Irish Sea dowses my face with rain
and stonechats call into the wind
which smells of cedar, coccus scarlet and hyssop.

If I return from the sea and wait in the marshes I will find
something soaking (*lean*), something pulled down from
the fells in the River Waver, moonlit florets of hogweed
drifting into the swamps. A white orchid folded into its
long paper leaves. Ribwort tight in an orbit of dreams.
Time to move like a deer to the end of the river, bud to
the edge of blossom, fresh in the taste of it, river meeting the salt marsh and dragging the pondweed so deep
its long wrinkled leaves are like feathers. Spittles of wax
in the ponds. Show me the seed, the small wheat caught
in gel waiting like a silver pin. Let me watch, small sharp
sea rush at my feet, long three-flowered rush at my back,
its flute-stems intoning with the rasp of salt (*reach, arms
forward*). And in the early dawn, it's the woodrush that

shows the first green, its roots parting to the glint of a
small pool, inclined for the capture; for the pull of a lover
into quick-water, into pleat, into spluttering bindweed,
turned and bound, gagged, sunk, hair splayed, then rest-
ing into fresh, bottomless glint of seed eye.

PROCESSION

From the west door
I follow the aisle to kneel,
head bowed, in front of the altar.

Above the Cross, the waves part
for the resurrected Christ,
ropes of fire pouring
through his pierced palms,
his arms so wide
they reach into the dome;

on his right, Mary
watches from the fields,
offering a sheaf of wheat,
the three lilies
in the hem of her dress
as bright as candles;

on his left, Elisabeth
steps from a forest,
water running from her hands,
the three roses
in the hem of her dress
as bright as coals.

I will walk to the east,
place both hands on the altar,
lean into the stone, and kiss.

Let it be that I kneel to tie an old sedge rope around a white oak, its trunk split and half-fallen, soft and dark splintered into the swamp. And that I bind my feet so that I can reach through woodrush and lean into the swamp towards him. My father, fresh water in my mouth for him to drink while he struggles, face like a slim bough just above the water, rose petal on a lake, legs kicking, bound into one. I will try not to cry into his eyes; they will be full of sky, blinking to stay open.

(Reach. And the song is.
Reach long for grasses soaked into the hem.)

He is a small white burnet rose,
a cheek turned in surprise,

a child lifted to hang
from sunken branches,
their stems pierced clean through
soft chapped bark,
the trunk silent in fissured coal,
a crumble of black wheels,

his drink is whisky rings,
earth and peat repeating,
dark-streams beneath the ice

his drink is sticky bud to frost,
remembering

(and when we bow)

EUCHARIST

**I will place the corporal
in the centre of the altar,
turn its single linen square
and unfold it four times.**

**I will smooth its nine squares
so that they lie as one
and the triple lip of the hem
is true to the edge of the stone.**

You walked here, Pa, storms washing into the Waver over Binsey Fell and through Throstles Nest. Birdsfoot, yellow rattle and fireweed at your feet, fiddling with vetch as you arrived, looking up in surprise at the marshes, river splitting into so many veins it was almost blood. The back of your jumper made you seem vulnerable, shuffling through the reeds, shoulders hunched, losing your way, looking to the sky as if blind, feeling you deserve to – suddenly – fall. Weeping sharp in your eyes. The ice-cold water is shocking, but right. And you sink, bindweed and clotted sedge soaking you in, folding your life. Your cry is an abandoned child weeping at tragedy, at burn, at stain, and still you kick, keep running, good morris-dancing boy, leaping across the town, white handkerchief swooped to the right side, to the left. Cross-step and jump, your ankle bells in time, stick bells high, ribbon wings, pleating all the way to the tower for cake, glint of swamp haunting you, pushing you into streets, houses, ink. And the sharp sea rush and pondweed binding is right, though you kick, wanting. And the glue of bent and jellied heath sedge is right, though you kick, asking if helplessness can be lifted, held, loved. If sinking is a penance that can be paid without life. Bound to love. Dark hair splayed in thin water above, your cheeks now a young man's, carefully breathing, sylph lodged in you like an arrow, orange and pewter sunset of your heart warming her. Myrrh and thin-petalled dog roses somewhere just out of sight in the long spreads of wide-leaved bushes on the shore. Your 'Let's get it right,' 'Come on, let's walk through the town and see who we meet,' dangles like the pendulum of an old oak clock. Grandfather Harry teaching you how to make it balance, then swing to tick. Your shoulder pressed against brick, the red brick alleyways and terrace houses you ran through as a boy, old allotments, wash-houses and pubs, running to help Harry with his heavy lawnmower in the parks, his hedge clippers, maybe get him to play a tune on the harmonium. But you sink, a gritty weight pushing in, your arms stuck, face to the sky, spluttering, hands tied to your sides. You think that if you let go, stopped reaching to stay above the waterline, your shoulders will sink, seeping into lost marsh, jumper billowed, closed-eyed fright, bones mixed with rotted driftwood – and you would. But you kick, loving, despite the pull, steel loving, the sky white above you as you then hold straight, obedient.

.

EUCHARIST

Two purificators
thin as bandages
will be folded and placed
towards the high windows

of the north,
their stitched red crosses
laid close to the hem
of the unwavering east

We are like two books folding their pages into one
another (*thin as bandages*). We are shoes in a row. My
small hands hold to your coat-tail, following in the fells,
together in silence. 'Walk ahead,' you say, and when I get
to the first peak I look back to you, almost bowed into
your thoughts, while I balance along the narrow dip of
the ledge, then start the next climb, your thoughts still
soaked, eyes to the rock, then looking upward to a clear
sky, wincing as if there is rain on your face, slowly focus-
ing on my gaze and, with a crack, you push towards me
like a storm ready to rage to the top, run.

I will lean in again and feed you with crushed berries.
A piece of apple and you will bite into it as if it's life,
remembering the kitchen in your dressing gown, tearing
over the pages hungry to read, though your memories will
be so bright they will be more than candle-lit, more than
sun. I will hover (*like a careful stitch*), reminding you of
the time you took me rowing on Derwentwater, 'Oh it'll
be fine, be fun', storm blowing in. You strained against
the waves, belting old mariner songs in the rain to keep me

from fear, my small wet hands clinging to the seat. I will describe your study in the cottage, small coal fireplace, low ceiling and beams. Rows of Wordsworth, Coleridge and Lawrence behind your desk, miner's lamp and low window in front. The evening light when sunset creeps across our lawn after rain and fills the room with amber. Keep walking in the fells, Pa, keep waiting (*bare side to the east*), I don't know how or what Maman will look like, but something of her will come.

EUCHARIST

**The gold paten
will be centred like a compass,
its wheel-cross emblem
turned to the east;**

**one damascened chalice
set to its north-west,
the other to its south-west,
their bare sides to the cross.**

Oh, Pa, it can be tiring in the unspoken words. Bruised reeds in a clatter of bids. We step forward together for life and bare-knuckle box our hearts to find out what's there. Another blow

to your chin from the city, a blow to my back from the home.
You took pain to show you were stronger. I tried to show it was
movable. Strike, and the grass is on water, not soil.

And we reached the peaks, bullocks to the chase, swarming on
the tops, arms nailed to the battering of wind, sucking the sight
of it, falcons to the tide.

Maybe love is a heavenly 'yes'; nurture and thirst; the holy
waters that baptise us into the desert, even when we are des-
tined to leave our bodies in the wilderness, our heads severed
and danced for as the price of power, maybe love runs clear with
the worthy and unworthy: a bright belief in us, companioning,
regretting our fall; a dark belief in us, knowing our abandoned
souls are whole and to be greeted as family; maybe love is simply
there and we push into the storm to make sure it's not a roman-
tic balm; we fight to allow ourselves to receive the earthly 'yes'
into our bones. Maybe it stands before us when we die and is in
that moment intoxicating.

EUCHARIST

The round wafer
fired with a wheatsheaf
will be placed on the paten;
wine will be poured

into the chalice turning
black in its silver,
and a cross of water
made in the wine.

Pa, will you find it worse to know or will it bring a moment of
*relief (*wild dark eye*)? Will it lift your guilt or will you grieve*
more? If I could write to you on paper that had solace in the
*ink, I would (*trace the hem*). It doesn't answer everything. She*
should have been heard. Should have been heard. With empty
hands, all I have is to sit with you by the fire and tell you, or give
you this letter to read while I wait respectfully outside. Her death
*certificate says sleeping pills (*trace*), but below, in a different sec-*
tion, it says 'a large quantity of an antidepressant found'. This
drug was taken off the market in 1971 because it produced a high
percentage of hallucinations and suicides. Her analyst must have
prescribed it and taken it herself. Carmen didn't like pills. She
was the only one of the three who survived. Maman must have
thought in all her heartbreak she was going mad. And she was.

PURIFICATORS

Within the white square
the two purificators
will be draped like folded veils

over the bread, over the wine.
Each will have their place.
And beneath the altar stone
is the dark nook bound
with the nard of Mary,
thread of Lazarus,
river of Elisabeth,
tied into the proscenium
of the starless shadow-theatre
and beneath the hem
of its hidden curtain
are the stone flags,
then the cornerstone,
then the earth.

LAVABO

I will turn to the north
and hold out my crossed hands
for water to be poured through
into the lavabo dish,
while I pray – I will that thy will.

When I turn again to the altar,
I will take a half-step back
and with thumb and forefinger

trace the hem of the corporal,
the line of the lip – thy will –

before I step forward and begin.

INVOCATION

The palms of my hands
will be together in prayer
– O Lord lift up our hearts –
and with an inbreath
I draw them upwards
to a flame above my head
– let us hold thy presence –
and my arms will open to rest
in a wide arc
of the Cross and Resurrection
as I incant across the altar
O Lord open thou our lips;

the words will rise with the dust
in the light-shafts
from the high nave windows
and settle in the putlock holes
of the old stone walls
like roosting doves

until they swoop on grey threads
from one dark hole to another,
beating the sound of our prayers.

BENEDICTUS

At the word Benedictus
like a veil at a wedding
the linen will be lifted
from the chalice and paten
their new metals shining

The circle of wafer
is held in both hands
and I will tell the story over it

we meet

white circle of time
white hole

to the Last Supper
sphere

of the gift

we meet
His word

and our word
His hands
and mine

and the song is

'On the night he was betrayed,
he took the bread and gave You thanks'

and the song is

'he broke it, saying "Take, eat;
this is my body given for you."' (*step forward, step*)

I will raise the bread
sun-like
arms lifted
through the black arc
the black noise
dark eye –
O da'at of the unwoven
dismantle us
between love and Love

bell

         bell

                  bell

after the after-ring
the resurrected body
of Christ will be borne

to the centre of the paten
and I will place my hands
within the corporal

palms down and bow
to one knee, heart infolded
robes crumpled below the altar

arms stretched above my head
towards the body of Christ
as if to a rock-ledge

we meet

and the song is

'on the night he was betrayed
he took the cup and gave You thanks'

and the song is

'he gave it to his disciples saying
"this is my blood."''
(*step back, step*)

I will raise the chalice
through the black arc
and hold its well of wine

purple iris, black rose

bell bell

                bell bell

                                bell bell

hand

                hand

                                kneel

my spine is a riverbed of stones
bowed into the silt and the sand and the grit
for the blood-river

to pour down

    'by whom'

        the bread
        is held above

           'and with whom'

               the wine
               and lifted

           'and in whom'
              given

   three bound to one axis

             'in the unity of the Holy Spirit'
             (to kneel is to rise)

        'all honour and glory be Yours'

        and the song is

This is   This is   This is blood. The spill of
                            rose-petals down the aisle

This is

wafer   arc lamp sweeping   the sea

This is

turned in hell

the raised scarred body

O beloved

body and the   blood   this

is rain   from river returned to

river

from river

silver   **wine-kiss on skin**   hand

hand

on the right side of the altar

and the left   hand in life   and   without

life

iris

this

is   death-linen   stretched   caul   vernix

drawn

            high and

              all   **heads drenched**

                all   **heads drenched**

                  all   heads drenched

                     O beloved

this   bloody milk

    this   **this**   **is**

Take.   **Eat.**   **Take.**   **Eat.**

there is   no more   **there is**   . no more

       these wings   this climb

                this

                 descent

     holy water   **pours**   *and the song is*

                   and the song is

We kneel in line, mouths open
We kneel   mouths open
We kneel in line mouths open. This

stamens reach
into the furnace to dip and twist and lift
full bulbs of molten glass ready to be blown

O beloved
there is a river under the stairs

roses and bracket fungus seep and ooze and spread and fan
from the side of the altar
their flood of scent distilled into calcite
bleeding milk-sap
with ancient nard and rose-oil dripping slow as amber
from the stone

there is a river under the stairs
O my beloved

Let us bend, Maman, like circles, even though we are wounded (*bow*). Return to the altar again. And let you see a slim Solway brook carving through creeping bent and mat grass, remembering, childlike, how sunlight is as fluid as the streams. Let it be that your mind follows the water as taut in its curves as a violin. And that the melody brings love to your thoughts, even if broken, still love. Let your glass-blue eyes watch. Let your careful feral hands gather black bog rush, hair tails and sea club rush, and let you be far into the swamps for a while, breeze lifting your hair, gathering long stems of chalk and fox sedge, whose brown shivering seeds scatter the earth. A distant sound of storm.

I'm looking for small marsh orchids (*lean forward*), parting reeds to see how the under-grass matts, and if I can find strings of grass from years before. The water is cold. I keep suckling my fingers to warm them and go in again to tease out the threads. And then something makes me flinch and look behind, my back straightened to see flecks above the swamps. They rise like sand shaken upward, like the distant movement of many, and in the shapes I suddenly see you beyond the wood, Maman, steel-eyed, watching.

EUCHARIST EXTENSION

People wait to the west without hope
        with hope
                buried in hope
for the slow procession
of altar unbound and rebound,
dried earth sifting from the hem of my cassock,
to pew, home, field and desert
where a soft voice or touch
on their shoulder
reminds them to open their mouths
heads back heart
seized (no matter what burn
from the merciless love
of the wild dark eye)
to the weightless vaulted heavens
for love to love for love

Your right shoulder is hunched, half-ready to pounce.
I lean into the hard rush, mud rush. Dog-like for a
moment, can I catch you? No. But you're waiting. Run
low, run through the reeds and I will be lost at your
heels. Run straight and my swinging stride will tip over
the bogs, plunge and trip. Run wild and I won't see. Only

your head moves, slightly, bird-like, luminous eye above sturdy bent thighs, feet poised. Your pierced focus, tracking me as if in conversation. I stand up, off balance for a moment, and then walk purposeful steps, navigating the clumps to make long strides as if walking down an aisle. Tall bulbs of reedmace tapping my shoulders like drums. Purple iris in hand, its long sheath of leaf surrounding yellow eyes. I'm hoping to steady you with the sight of it, until I hear your moan, a drone of pre-pipes as if your ears are full and your throat joins the tremor.

HYMN

to return

to the east

to stone

to linen

to chalice

to paten

to caul

to wax

to flame

to shadow

to river

to stone

to earth
to bow
to the east
to return

A jolt to the chest, flick of hand, breath to belly, spark to cheek, ready? Run (*run*)! And morning calls with its carpet damp on moulded stairs, floors broken through the night, my small jaw leaning, repeating, growing heavy and square. Sliced light seen only in silver, in tin. Legs bent almost to splinter and break, mould fur creeping up my shins, onto my thighs, heels lifting and run, run without sight, hoofs clampering, height rising. Vault over spears of great woodrush, kick back, dive, jolt. Your eye meets me faster, closer, like a stream. Iris thrown to the ground, offerings strewn without words, I'm finding you, your chest widening, both shoulders rising, breasts taut and bare, thick leather skin, our arms holding the air as if it were ribbons, slosh of water, swamp drum, we're close, shape to shape and you turn, eye to the ground like a start gun, greyhounds in wait – and we're off, canter, jump, lift – scatter with the starlings, roar into the heights, our wild screams bound in the wind. I've found you, laughing.

(And the song is. And the song is stretched into a bow; arrows arched full as blood; a pierced eye (look up) ready to surrender.)

TOP ALTAR CLOTH

The cloth will be imprinted
from the chalice and paten
its sides drawn in equally,
five crosses for five wounds;
the four red at each corner,
now piled to the sides,
the white fifth, front and centre
holding firm against the tide
the lace around the edges
meeting like thousands of shells

I can dribble water into my father's mouth, but it's only Maman who can lean in to get him; and she's there, Pa, you can't turn your head to see, almost drowned, but she is behind you, nearly too late, unable to find you. She's not in the spread of sylphs, the hundreds shaking their small round bells with tufted hair, velvet bent and canary grass. She's not in the spread of water nymphs diving, skating through the streams; she is tall with piercing eyes, she is from days of deserts baked in heat, defying the sand;

nights in the forest, learning her name, wild voice, drone (*and the song is*). She was on the other side of the wall, weeping. She was on the stairs, regretting, as frightened as we were. She was at the door when you arrived, on fire with guilt. She was fierce in her surrender, charging to the heavens to find forgiveness, to find her way back. She is bigger, Pa, wilder, stronger. Reed pipes in blossom, breasts bare, no lady's bow, only reverence given carefully, slicingly, eyes in full sight. And she is reaching strong muscled arms into the swamp for you, through the rain of last year and the year before, past the mud, she is hook-nailed, clawing into the silence, full of life, the sleeves of her woollen jumper rolled up, pulling out the stench of slime and frogspawn, your charred feet in old wood.

And the suction brings a tide, your skin like glue in her arms, coughing into her chest. And the tide passes the line of the Solway shore bringing boulders of blue rocks, cave rocks, stone eggs, no nails. And the eggs will never float, they will roll out of the sea and crack open to live in the sun, split into spindles, carved crystals, never having been full, always space between their shards waiting to be laid out in their shapes across sands and marshes, as if they're listening to the layers underneath the grass, under the floors, the stairs, the roofs. As if they are themselves, loud.

FAIR LINEN

exact to the altar
exact to the ground
rolled never folded
a circular prayer
sealed in its hem
shema israel adonai
elohaenu adonai ehad
shema israel adonai
elohaenu adonai ehad
sealed in its hem
a circular prayer
rolled never folded
exact to the ground
exact to the altar

Maman, if you left for the Desert Mothers and wept in their arms, fasted in their sands, healed in their caves, you took something of me with you. Or is it that they came to me and surrounded my prayers, my silence, my service, so that I might learn how to manage thirst?

Let it be that the mistral has passed and the skies are clearer than glass. Let us return to the chapel garden by the broken wall and watch the Alps beyond Mount Lure show their pillars and domes in a glint of white pink, before they return to cloud. Mars, Venus, Saturn and the Milky Way so close we feel ourselves peering from the sphere of earth. Meteorites shooting from east to west. A cratered moon lifting the moths, the shadow swallows and the water in the well, which we drink.

THE HOURS

Stillness after the Eucharist

LAUDS

There is a seal in the horizon
that splits
with the sharp inbreath
of afternight and the day to come.
Creation drawn back into its creation
before the furious inrush of light
to be re-named, re-met, re-loved as the beloved
lip of the dawn.

PRIME

Above the heavens
is a sphere of such ferocious praise
that if you listen
you will hear silence,
while the angels repeat one word
in so many forms they need no other language,
but in the first hour after dawn
one note steals through
the edge of hearing
moving towards us and away,
a claw of yearning
joined by three, then five, then seven
to pull the bark-lines into skyward ladders again,
to scatter the early spray of waterfalls
into vectors and prisms
and shake the soil past the clay and the peat
to its matted underbells.

We sit in the tomb
and wait for the first handprint
the first voice
that becomes our chant
in the shadows of the cave
and our call
at the mouth of the cave
where we rest by a stoup carved into the rock
to wet our throats
into song
and then step
into the garden
longing for our names
(Mary, do you know me)
and finding them in the ballads of others
make new tales of them
until they are no longer ours
and we return
(do you know me)
to the tomb
and wait for the first

We meet like Mary and Elisabeth
flames above our heads and in our bellies
the dreams we tell lengthening
to a high chorale
our Tower of Babel brought into the temple
for all visions
to be poured on to the altar
like water into a vast silver bowl
its singing chalice
in the hot and silent noon
a lake-mirror of mountain and sky
circling to open its centre
so the small nook
of the soul
bound in mud and silt
under the altar
is magnified

NONES

we bring spikenard
to the shore of Galilee
(bride returning)
to anoint
his feet
water to wine to oil
and dry them with our hair
long after
the fishing boats have been moored
and the dawn fire
(bride returning)
has become a charcoal oven

VESPERS

The thread came
as a plumb line
through heavy grey clouds
clear
and soft
in its slow descent
heard as one note
the evening thermals circling
its straight fall as if it were an anchor-chain
descending
from the great ship
towards her upturned face
palms open
her body so still
it was almost clay
while the long translucent wire
passed her cheek
and burned
then kissed her mouth
this is my body
to split her throat into
many throats

her belly opened
as every blood rose
and her heart
gathered
with all weak and broken nests
to be slit and sewn
by this searing filament
of praise

COMPLINE

in the fissure of sleep
is a narrow path
through earth and rock
past three iron bells
each the width of four altars
each bound in frayed ropes of woody rosemary
rust and evergreen concealed in the dark
like a wreath
creation drawn back into its creation
and under their broad shuddering rims
there are three sheafs
(keep me in the darkness of your eye)
of wild poppies, purple iris, lavender and black figs
their bruised opiates
infusing the earth
and the soles of our feet
as we descend
to the silent toll

And, beloved, when, on my silent retreat I knelt,
bowed and laid to the ground before your altar,
in the cave, by the white wall
I found that I loved you

                                    not because you lay
                and knelt with me, my every blood in your hands
                       but that you reminded me of the beauty
                                in the mountains

and in the sea and that your every care
and furious strength
gave me peace

                                it was then that I knew
                            your humble blood was in mine

ST BEGA'S

We walk along a wooded path (*step forward*) towards old St Bega's Church on Bassenthwaite Lake. When the tides were low it stood at the shore, but now it's on an island in the middle. Water glazed around it. A pewter mirror under the blaze of sunset. The island's face lifted to shafts of orange in yellow and blood red, life red, our red. We stand at the edge, crunch of pebbles underfoot, three in a row, watching. The woods are at our backs – *Ah, another garden* – and then, as the bell rings, we wade in. The boat was loosened in the night's storm, left to the tide; it waits cupped in colour: petal on a lake. All three of us push forward, cold water to defiant thighs. I see you now, my mother, scarred throat, new strong back, chorus of dawn like a fanned fire behind you, delicate fingers. You pull the water to splash your face before you swim. I see you, my father, burnt eyes, the sound of hymns belted into the wind, cairn to your side and your song reaching for the far-off peaks like a balm. Books now read in the kitchen as psalms.

When we row, wet sleeves and glass faces, we pull the oars like a heartbeat.

At the church we are three in a pew. Light streaks through the windows, showing dust circling to climb and return. Dust to dust. My hand is vulnerable, it's open, like the inside of an egg; closer now, can see the skin of it. Maman smells familiar, washed curls, woollen jumper. She paints and writes, bracelet to her wrist. I sketch and write. Pa writes and then paces through the arches in debate. Rock and trees carved with Celtic prayers. The lake joining others from the east like a river towards the sea. Pa is still a little wet. He takes a candle out of a wooden box. Its ready wick is still in wax. At first it struggles to keep the flame. He has to hold a match to it for a while as it changes shape. It needs relighting. We stay through the evening, sometimes eating fruit. Pa sucks vanilla vetch or has a loud bite of an apple. The candle needs to be relit many times. There is the scent of something like roses in the air. Just before dark, starlings fly so close to the window they seem slow, like glowing fish. Their mouths are berry-full, returning to nests. When I give these letters to you both, I will kneel, arms stretched towards the altar like a bridge *(and the song is) and the song is*.

LAVARE

I catch the swing of the pendulum
in its dark rosewood case
and gently hold its quietening
until it rests its brass heart at the meridian.
I light two candles on the dresser
the belly and tip of their flames are drawn upwards
by an almost-thread of black smoke
until I close the curtains into a wine-like shadow
that brings the stillness of the night over Bassenthwaite.

Our hearts have ceased and outpour, O my beloved,
you lie between death and her sister sleep
both turned towards you, dark-eyed –
one strokes your arm, the other's hands are cupped,
holding a balm of sweet heavy milk to your eyes
ready for the river.

On the small oak table beside the bed
a scoured brass bowl sits
with a white egg cup and a glass jug,
each in its own orbit
each with its own open-rimmed sound,

three small inbreaths, three receivers,
the water in the jug curved
in its still meniscus.

My sisters left these vessels before dawn, O my beloved,
as they lay with you;
they placed them on the table
through Ain Soph, Ain Soph Aur,
through nothingness into brokenness
through the blood, the blade, the linen
before they were washed into their clean shapes
like the first and last flowers.

By the jug are three white cotton cloths
their stitched red crosses in line.
Large enough to wring, thick enough to soak,
strong enough to be returned to the bowl,
soaked and wrung, soaked and wrung again.
In a small leather box is a blue glass phial of rose oil
its silver top scuffed and worn back to lead
and a thumb-size pot of chrism.

My sisters are two and many, O my beloved,
a chain of women's hands turning the phial,
turning my hands, a rose of hands,
crown upon crown of nard and chrism,

of callous and scar all brought to your skin
with such precision, such tenderness.

I lift the jug to pour its waterfall
drinks the stillness back into its stream,
back to the source which prays to Mount Lure
before it falls again in spheres of all sizes
their glass skins diving, water to water,
into the clear pool to rise,
a momentary ring of silver froth
that mirrors the bronze circle below.

**Their palms are pierced with the river of Elisabeth,
O my beloved:
one hand to the heavens for a rush of fire
the other turned, palm-down, to yield a mountain stream.
You can hear the water like a lithophone over the boulders
it echoes through the shingle
and runs towards the grass banks in the sun.
My sisters are the water-bearers of the Jordan,
shore-whisperers of Galilee,
they are the balm that Elisabeth brought
to bathe her dead son.**

The egg cup is three-quarters full
of warm milk, still as porcelain.

I pour a few drops that fall heavy
and deep into the water,
complete for a moment,
then open like white smoke
into soft hands spreading.

They bear the sheaf of Mary, O my beloved,
their bellies swollen with harvest,
their breasts heavy with the milk of life and afterlife,
singing the lullaby of compline.

The oil is olive and rose;
eleven slow brown drops
lie on the surface like lilies rooted to the base.
As I bless the water and stir
they become a thousand beads, a thousand eyes
breaking open a scent richer than gardens
until the altar fills our shadow room.

Their hair is wet with the oils of the Unnamed, O beloved:
the perfume of the women who wash the newborn
knowing they will become old; who wash the dead
knowing they were once children;
who dry our tears, bathe our wounds,
anoint the feet of strangers.

I take a cloth in both hands
and lower it into the milky water,

not to bathe you, ready for the mark
of another new morning, but as an offering.
My hands knock the sides of the brass bowl
to the low memory of a bell
and the first linen is wrung out
streaked with rose, like earth or old blood,
and laid warm on your shoulder.

Oh my beloved, you are in the reed basket
at the water's edge where the three sisters,
ferrywoman, death and sleep
have set you down in the shallows
to wash you into the river;
we have placed the wafer of the Eucharist on your tongue,
mouth closed; a drop of wine in each hand,
palm open, and a rose petal over each eyelid.

I lift the hair from your forehead
as I bathe your brow. The rim of your ear
is tender, and the skin of your arm
still soft enough to respond
as if you were asleep, though the angle
of your elbows and knees is unusually geometric,
especially when moved. There is little wax;
that will come later, and glaze the porcelain
that slowly fills your face. Your hands
curling inwards, over hours, as if held.

O beloved, the sisters swim into the tide with you
and set your basket carefully between the twin currents
of law and mercy
while along the banks the roots and seeds
of iris, foxtail and sedge
burst with discernment.
Each fierce stream would pull you to its own course
but the central tide of forgiveness
painfully threads itself through a river-swarm of buds
rushing into bloom.
Some lean and rest on the rocks, petals loose,
some catch in the reeds or matt crimson into the willow,
some racing with the bore.
All your old masks and second eyes
are washed away
with last year's bark and confetti,
while the riverbed is carved and contoured
by your deepest loves
which chart the movement of your bones.

Your body has found its final shape.
I sweep across your skin and I follow the kite-tails
of wrinkles gathering ahead of my cloth
I wash the cheek I kissed goodnight
the shoulder that I fell asleep on
the arms that carried dried flowers home

the finger that wore a slim gold ring
the hands that painted shells
and pointed sternly to the truth
the crook of the elbow I snuck into on the sofa
while you had long, grown-up conversations
the chest that wheezed under your woollen jumper
the belly that gave birth to me
the thighs that knelt in bed to read with me
the hands that fed me before I could hold
and loved me before I could love
the feet that walked barefoot on the beach
while we collected shells in the wind.
I bathe your feet and hold them
I bathe your feet and hold them.

O beloved, the breath of the divine body
is in your mouth, the blood surrender in your hands,
the lament of Mary around you, washed into the waves;
her ballad is every story, and every story is broken
on the water into new songs,
a million fire-mirrors
that hold and change, reconcile and reconcile:
and somewhere the wide sea now gathers you to itself,
river-Christ to your right, lake-Christ to your left, sea-Christ
reaching to take your every error, every grief or joy
and draw you into the vision of Mary, the song of Elisabeth,

and the stillness of Christ's compassion
as they surrender under the round sky.

It is only left for me to bow.
The bowl is a quarter-full, the wet cloths folded.
And when we pleat we bind, crossing through and under.
With my forefinger I take chrism from the gold pot
and anoint your eyelids, forehead, lips,
and then your heart.
I take your right hand in mine and rub small circles
into your palm, and then the left.
My hair falls loose as I anoint the soles of your feet.

O beloved

you are

gift

you are

taken

you are

mother

sister

bride

Christ

thou art

God

Yahweh

Elohim

holy one

thou art

one

ACKNOWLEDGEMENTS

In gratitude to my grandmothers Mary Ethel Bragg, Andre Roche, Elsie Roche. My great grandmothers Hannah Bragg, Mary Jane Bragg, Bell Park, Mrs Gilbertson, Mary Cunradi, Marie Josephine Roche. My god-mothers Poh Sim Plowright, Jay Wheldon, Cynthia Jonson. My great aunts Mary Stephens, Elsie Bragg, Shirley Bragg, Margaret Miller, Ada Hocking, Barbara Hocking and Margaret Hocking, Noemi Colette Cunradi, Laure Marcelle Cunradi; my aunts Andre Roche, Dadou Roche, Josette Roche. My surrogate aunts Carmen Callil, Caroline Blomfield, Carol McKay. My mother's friends Joan Murphy, Virginia Powell, Julia Matheson. And my grandmother's best friends Jean Morrison and Jean Connolly.

Thank you also to Mimi Khalvati, Piers Plowright, Mark Chapman and Rowan Williams for their guidance, and Barbara Turner Vesselago.

Finally, I am very grateful to Clara Farmer and Peter Straus for their support; Greg Clowes for his assistant editing; Rosie Palmer for the beautiful cover; and for the thoughtful companionship of my editor Poppy Hampson who is nothing less than a gift.

GLOSSARY

Ain – Nothing.

Ain Soph – Limitlessness.

Ain Soph Aur – Unending light.

– The three veils of creation described in Judaeo-Christian mysticism.

Alb – White linen tunic.

Alpha – First letter of the Greek alphabet.

Amice – White cloth with two long ribbons.

Anoint – The use of precious oils to bless, often used in a rite of passage.

Benedictus – Form of blessing, usually used at the beginning of an invocation.

Cassock – Full-length garment, generally black, derived from monastic clothing.

Censed – To ritually bless or cleanse with the odour of burning incense.

Chalice – Ceremonial cup or goblet used in the Eucharist.

Chrism – Consecrated oil used for baptism, anointing the dying, and other rites.

Cincture – Monastic belt made of rope for the alb.

Communicant – Person who takes the sacraments.

Communion – To take the sacraments.

Cope – Embroidered cape worn by a priest or bishop.

Corporal – Linen cloth on which the chalice and paten are placed during the Eucharist.

Da'at – The window between worlds. A point of unification and communion.

Eucharist – The sacraments of a Mass.

Eucharist extension – The sacrament taken to the pews of a church or into a parish for those who are unable to attend the altar.

Host – The bread of the Eucharist.

Incipit – The first word of a text or chanted liturgy.

Invocation – Call to the presence of God.

Lavabo – Ceremonial jug of water used to cleanse, and a bowl to catch the water.

Lavare – Ceremonial washing.

Magnificat – Song of Mary when she meets Elisabeth and their babies leap for joy in their wombs (Luke 1:44–65).

Monstrance – Glass vessel used to exhibit the consecrated Host.

Paschal – Candle representing the risen Christ.

Paten – Ornamental plate used for bread during the Eucharist.

Penitent – Person who seeks forgiveness.

Purificator – White linen used to wipe the chalice after each communicant partakes.

Sacrament – The blessed or transformed bread and wine.

Shema Israel adonai – Central prayer in Judaism and Christianity:

> Shema Israel adonai
>
> elohaenu adonai ehad
>
> Hear, O Israel: the Lord
>
> our God, the Lord is one.
>
> – Deuteronomy (6:4) and Mark (12:29–31)

Stole – Silk vestment that marks recipients of Holy Orders.

Tabernacle – Cloth that covers and defines a sacred place.

Taper – Slim wax candle to light larger candles.

Thurible – Metal censer suspended from chains, in which incense is burned.